FORTNITE:
Building

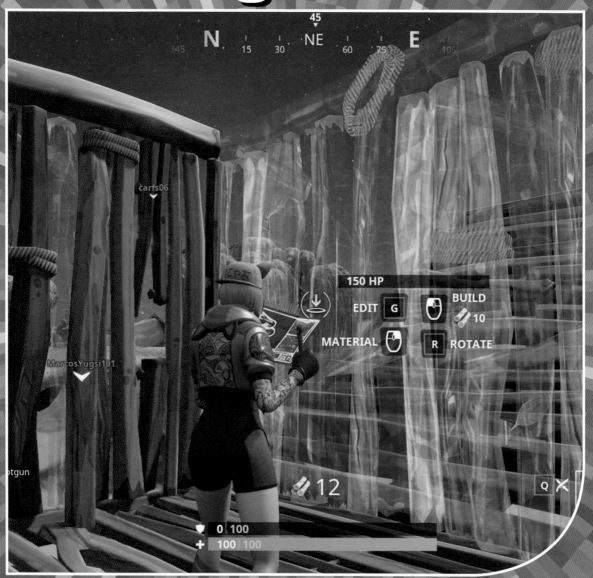

CHERRY LAKE PUBLISHING • **ANN ARBOR, MICHIGAN**

by Josh Gregory

Published in the United States of America by Cherry Lake Publishing
Ann Arbor, Michigan
www.cherrylakepublishing.com

Reading Adviser: Marla Conn MS, Ed., Literacy specialist, Read-Ability, Inc.

Library of Congress Cataloging-in-Publication Data
Names: Gregory, Josh, author.
Title: Fortnite. Building / by Josh Gregory.
Other titles: Building
Description: Ann Arbor, Michigan : Cherry Lake Publishing, 2019. | Series:
    Unofficial guides | Series: 21st century skills innovation library |
    Includes bibliographical references and index. | Audience: Grade 4 to 6.
Identifiers: LCCN 2019003340 | ISBN 9781534148123 (lib. bdg.) |
    ISBN 9781534150980 (pbk.) | ISBN 9781534149557 (pdf) |
    ISBN 9781534152410 (ebook)
Subjects: LCSH: Fortnite (Video game)—Juvenile literature.
Classification: LCC GV1469.35.F67 G743 2019 | DDC 794.8—dc23
LC record available at https://lccn.loc.gov/2019003340

Cherry Lake Publishing would like to acknowledge the work of the Partnership for
21st Century Learning. Please visit www.p21.org for more information.

Printed in the United States of America
Corporate Graphics

Contents

Chapter 1   **How Do They Do It?**   **4**

Chapter 2   **Putting the Pieces Together**   **10**

Chapter 3   **Combat Construction**   **18**

Chapter 4   **Getting Creative**   **26**

Glossary   **30**

Find Out More   **31**

Index   **32**

About the Author   **32**

Chapter 1

How Do They Do It?

Watching your favorite *Fortnite* **streamers** can be a lot of fun. The top players pull off amazing moves while chatting with fans and cracking jokes. They make it look easy as they

Diving into your first *Fortnite* match is a lot of fun, but getting really good at the game takes time and effort.

You might be battling another player, only for them to suddenly be safely behind metal walls high up in a tower.

smoothly build towers, take aim at rival players, and coast to victory. But when you try some of these same techniques while playing *Fortnite* with friends, you find out that it isn't quite as easy as you thought!

If you are only a *Fortnite* beginner, these top players might seem to have superhuman skills. They move impossibly fast. Tall towers can suddenly appear as if they have burst up from underground. Walls and ramps can spring up out of nowhere. If you are playing against someone who builds like this, you might suddenly find yourself boxed inside of a wooden room and unable to move. Or your rival might throw up a series of walls while dodging and suddenly pop up behind you with a surprise attack.

How do these players build so quickly without making mistakes? How do they know just what to build in different situations? Are they using magic powers? Of course not! They have simply practiced a lot and learned the ins and outs of *Fortnite* building. With the

You might see a screen like this a lot until you get good at building.

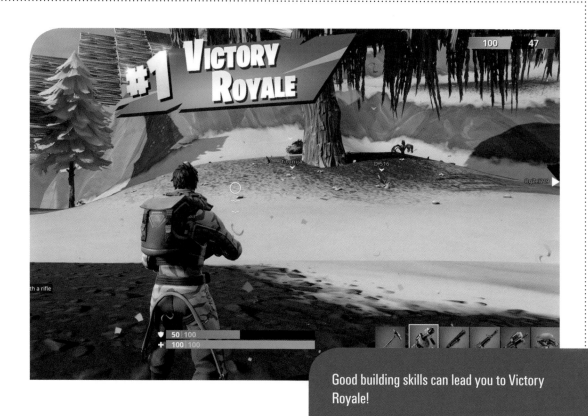

Good building skills can lead you to Victory Royale!

right tips and enough practice, you can become just as great a builder as any pro *Fortnite* star.

At first, it might seem like you could ignore the building part of *Fortnite*. In the early minutes of a match, you can probably get by with weapons and reflexes. But you'll soon find that all of the best *Fortnite* players are great builders. Building is what sets *Fortnite* apart from other competitive online battle games. You simply won't win very many matches, if any at all, without mastering your construction skills.

Building can help you do many things in *Fortnite*. You can use it to stay hidden or protect yourself from attacks. You can use it to sneak up on other players or attack them from unexpected angles. You can even use it to travel around the *Fortnite* island and reach new locations.

Need to climb a mountain? Just build a huge ramp.

Watch and Learn

If you are ever having trouble getting the hang of things in *Fortnite*, try watching how the pros play. After you get knocked out in a *Fortnite* match, you can watch from the eyes of the player who beat you. If that player is defeated, your view will switch to the player who defeated them. By the end of the match, you'll be watching the top player. This is a great way to learn new skills.

You can also watch streams or recordings of top *Fortnite* players in action. Sometimes these players will even explain their strategies as they play. This helps viewers learn more about the game as they watch.

But perhaps most importantly, building in *Fortnite* is a lot of fun. If you've ever played *Minecraft* or put together a Lego sculpture, you know how satisfying it can be to imagine something and build it just the way you want it. Let's dive into the world of *Fortnite* and get started!

Chapter 2

Putting the Pieces Together

The first thing you need to get started with building in *Fortnite* is a good supply of construction materials. After all, you can't build something from nothing. You will need plenty of wood,

It won't take long to find enough materials to build something simple.

When you see a chest or some other container, open it up. You never know what you will find inside!

stone, and metal first. Luckily, these materials are **abundant** in the world of *Fortnite*.

You'll want to **scavenge** for materials throughout the course of each *Fortnite* match you play. The more you can collect, the more you will be able to build. So how does scavenging work? There are three main ways you can fill your pockets with useful materials. First, you can find them lying on the ground or inside of containers such as crates or Supply Llamas. This method will not get you much, but every little bit helps when you are collecting materials. Another way to collect wood, stone, and metal is to defeat other players. When players are knocked out of the game, they will drop everything they were carrying. You can pick up all of it for yourself!

The best way to gather building materials is to use your pickaxe. All players are equipped with a pickaxe. You have it from the start of every match, and you cannot drop it. This useful tool can be used to break apart almost anything you see in *Fortnite*. Tear down

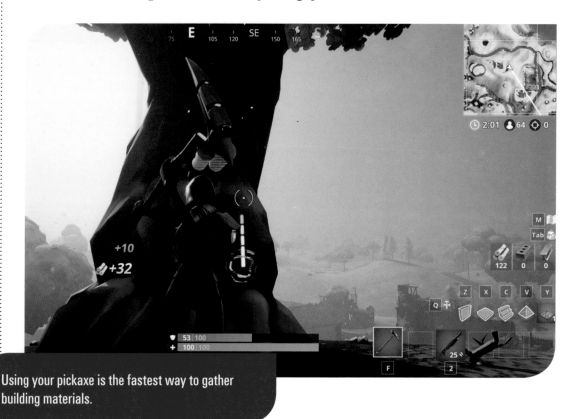

Using your pickaxe is the fastest way to gather building materials.

Each metal wall has 500 hit points, while wooden walls have 150. This means it takes more than three times as much damage to destroy metal.

the walls of houses. Break boulders apart. Smash parked cars. Every time you break one of these objects apart, it will give you building materials. As you swing your pickaxe, try to hit the blue circle that moves around on-screen. This will break things faster and earn you more materials.

The three building materials in *Fortnite* are each a little different. Knowing the right uses for each one is an important part of becoming a master builder. Wood is the weakest material. This means it is easier for enemies to destroy. However,

An Ever-Changing Game

The **developers** of *Fortnite* are always working to improve the game and make it more fun to play. One way they do this is by making small changes to better **balance** the game. For example, they might realize that one type of gun is far more powerful than the others. They could change the gun to make it a little weaker. This would balance the weapons.

Over time, the *Fortnite* developers have made several balance changes to the way building works in the game. They have changed the amount of materials needed to build different structures. They have also changed the amount of damage different materials can take before they are destroyed. Because *Fortnite* is always changing, you could log in one day to find out that things are a little different than you remember. When this happens, the only thing you can do is keep playing and learn to adjust to the changes!

you can build fastest with wood. This makes it perfect when you need to quickly throw up temporary walls or ramps. For example, if an enemy player starts shooting at you, you can rush to build a wooden wall to block the shots. (*Fortnite* veterans call this a "panic wall.") The wall doesn't need to last long. It just needs to offer some protection while you move to a better position.

Metal is the strongest material. However, it is very slow to build things out of metal. This means you should save it for when you need to build more permanent structures. Before you start building, make sure there are no rival players around. You don't want to get surprised as you slowly put up metal walls.

Stone is right in between wood and metal. It isn't the strongest or the weakest. It isn't the fastest or the slowest. This means it is useful in many different situations. But it is almost never the best choice if you have other materials available.

Once you have gathered some materials, you can start experimenting with *Fortnite*'s building system. You can build four main types of structures in the game. They are walls, floors, roofs, and stairs. These four pieces can be snapped together and arranged in almost any way you can imagine. They fit together on a **grid**. Simply aim at different spots to choose where you want to build. You can also press a button to rotate the structure. Before you build, you will be able to look at a see-through version of the structure on-screen. This shows you where the structure will appear and what it will look like.

Each piece will pop into place as soon as you press the button to build it. This means you can instantly stand on new ramps or block bullets with new walls. However, the pieces will start out with low hit points. Hit points are the amount of damage they can take from enemy weapons before they are destroyed. They will slowly increase as the structure finishes building.

You might notice that there is a fifth square on the screen as you rotate between the four main structures

Before you place a trap, you will be able to see how big an area it will cover.

in your building menu. This square is for building traps. You can find and pick up traps scattered around the *Fortnite* island just like weapons or potions. They can be attached to your buildings, and they do not require materials to build.

As you play the game, you might come across some other building-related items. For example, the Port-a-Fort is an item that instantly builds a simple tower. This is useful for when you need defense but don't have time to build something yourself. You can also find items such as huge mounted guns, campfires that heal you, and floor pads that launch you into the air. These items can all be added to your forts.

By now, you should have a general idea of how building works in *Fortnite*. Now let's see how you can use those skills to help you win a match!

Chapter 3

Combat Construction

Learning how to put a structure together is only the beginning when it comes to building in *Fortnite*. After all, Battle Royale isn't a relaxed building game. It is a fast-paced, competitive action game. That means you probably won't get many chances to

Feel free to knock down a wall if you don't want to use the door!

Practice building simple forts until you can do it very quickly without making mistakes.

take your time and build carefully in a typical match. Instead, you'll need to be able to put things together on the fly as you dodge incoming attacks and mount your own offense.

When you first start playing, you will probably be a slow builder. This is OK. Speed and **accuracy** will come naturally with practice. First, get used to the controls by building some simple towers. At the beginning of a match, try parachuting into an area where there are few other players. Knock down some trees, rocks, or other objects. Then start building. Try to build a simple two-story tower. Then try to build a second one even faster. Repeat the process until you can throw down a basic tower in just a couple of seconds.

You should try to stay moving as much as possible in *Fortnite*. This is true even when you are building. Don't simply stand still as you place walls on the ground. As soon as you press the button to start building a piece, start moving toward the next piece. You can even jump as you build. This will let you climb a

Building ramps underneath yourself is a great way to get up high quickly.

Even if you are great at building in *Fortnite*, remember that other players can use all the same tricks against you. When two great builders face off against each other, they try to outsmart each other by doing unpredictable things. Think creatively as you build and fight. Which strategy do you think your opponent will expect you to use? Can you try something different?

You will likely meet plenty of players who can build much faster than you. But that doesn't mean you will lose the fight. Remember that all structures can be destroyed in *Fortnite*. Are your enemies hiding out in a tall tower? Knock it down!

tower as you construct it. Aim down and build a ramp near your feet, then jump just as it starts building. You should now be standing on the new ramp. Now add the next story of walls to your tower. Build another ramp and jump up. If you can master this process, you can quickly build yourself high into the air.

Practice building until you can create a variety of structures quickly and accurately while staying on the move. Once you can do this, you've got the hard part down. Now you just need to learn the right situations for building different things in *Fortnite*. After all, even the best builders won't get far if they are building the wrong things at the wrong time.

It is usually a bad idea to spend a lot of time building complex structures early in a *Fortnite* match. The storm eye shrinks on a different part of the island each match. You can't predict where it will go. This means you could spend a long time building a great tower, only to be forced to abandon it to escape the storm. Instead, save your big building for the end of a match. This will also give you more time to gather plenty of materials early in the match.

However, that doesn't mean you shouldn't build at all. Quickly building very small structures can help you in many situations in *Fortnite*. For example, imagine that an enemy player suddenly pops up from around the corner of a house and starts firing at you. One strategy is to throw up a panic wall as quickly as you can. It will provide cover and give you a chance to **flank** the opposing player.

Or imagine you are fighting against another player in a wide-open area with no cover. The enemy player has a long-distance sniper rifle. But you only have a shotgun. You need to close the distance between you. How do you do it? Try throwing out a ramp right in front of you. Climb it as it builds, then jump off the

When you want to get on top of something, building a quick ramp is often faster than taking the stairs.

front and immediately build another ramp. Repeat this process until you are closer to your enemy. The ramps provide cover from incoming shots. At the same time, you can keep moving forward. Another benefit is that it becomes harder for your enemy to aim at you as you move up and down from the ramps.

You can also build yourself into the air with a taller tower when fighting. If you are good at building, this will give you a huge advantage. First, your enemies will have a hard time seeing exactly where you are as you build. The walls of your tower will block their vision. But if they remain at ground level, you will likely be able to spot them from above. You can pop out of cover and fire your shot.

Basic towers and ramps are good for more than just combat. You can also use them to help you get around the *Fortnite* island. Want to reach the top of a steep mountain? Simply build a ramp up the side. Want a bird's-eye view of the map as you travel?

Build a shape like this at the top of your tower. It will give you cover while allowing you to peek out and fire your weapons.

Build up into the air, then place platforms to create a bridge in the sky.

When you are building simple, disposable structures like this, it is best to use wood. You want to build as quickly as you can, and it doesn't matter if the walls and ramps get destroyed. Save your stronger resources for building a big tower near the end of the match.

Once the match gets down to just a few players, go ahead and start building a stronger, taller fort. By now, the storm eye should be small. You will probably notice other players building forts of their own. Use metal or stone to build the bottom levels of your tower. If the lower levels get destroyed, the whole tower will fall. This means you want them to be as strong as possible.

At the highest point of your tower, consider building two ramps in a V shape. You can duck into the middle of the V when you need cover. You can also run up the ramps to peek out over the edge and fire at enemies.

Chapter 4

Getting Creative

Battle Royale can be a lot of fun. But do you ever wish there were a way you could spend time building a crazy fort without having to worry about enemy players or a shrinking storm circle? For a long time, this simply wasn't possible. *Fortnite* was all about competition, with little chance to explore the more creative parts of the game. This all changed

Select Game Mode:

SAVE THE WORLD   Co-op PvE
BATTLE ROYALE   100 Player PvP
CREATIVE   Explore. Play. Invent.

Cooperative PvE storm-fighting adventure!

Fortnite fans were thrilled to see a third mode added to the main menu of the game.

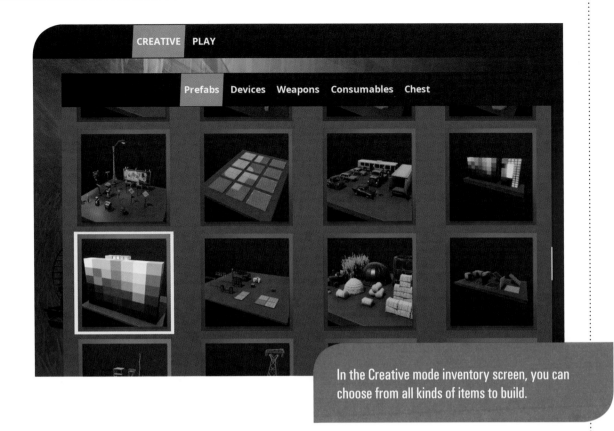

In the Creative mode inventory screen, you can choose from all kinds of items to build.

in December 2018 with the launch of a brand-new *Fortnite* mode.

In Creative mode, players get their very own *Fortnite* islands to play with. When you start a new game in Creative mode, you will find yourself on a small, mostly empty island with no other players. But you might notice that you have unlimited amounts of all three building materials. This means you can make whatever you want without anyone bothering you!

You might also notice that the **inventory** screen in Creative mode looks a lot different than it does in

Battle Royale. Here, you can choose from many different pre-built objects you can add to your island. Want to quickly toss out a huge castle or a pile of old cars? Go ahead! You can also equip any weapon or item in the game at any time. This means you can experiment, practice, or just play around.

You don't have to worry about taking damage when you fall from high places in Creative mode. In fact, you can even fly around if you want to. Tap the

You can spy on your enemies from behind the walls you build. Simply highlight a wall and choose to edit it. You can now see through it, but your enemies can't!

Shapes and Sizes

Each main building piece in *Fortnite* can be edited to form different shapes. For example, a standard wall is three squares wide and three squares tall. You can remove squares to add windows or doors, or to make a shorter wall to use as a fence. Or you could turn a basic ramp into a spiral staircase. In Battle Royale mode, making these kinds of changes can cost you valuable time. Many players choose to ignore the edit feature. However, it is very useful in Creative mode. Here, you can use it to make shapes that would otherwise be impossible. Experiment and see what you can come up with!

jump button twice to take flight. This lets you zoom around the island so you can build more easily.

Unlike in Battle Royale, the things you build in Creative mode are saved when you exit the game. This means you can keep building and improving your work each time you play. Once you have things the way you like them, you can invite friends to join your island.

Like Battle Royale, Creative mode is a work in progress. The *Fortnite* developers are always working to improve the game and add new features. Keep playing to see what they do next!

Glossary

abundant (uh-BUHN-duhnt) widely available in large amounts

accuracy (AK-yuh-ruh-see) a measurement of how correct or precise something is

balance (BAL-uhns) to make a game more fair or fun to play by making adjustments to the rules

developers (dih-VEL-uh-purz) people who make video games or other computer programs

flank (FLANGK) to attack an enemy from the side

grid (GRID) a system of lines that intersect to form many squares

inventory (IN-vuhn-toh-ree) a list of the items your character is carrying

scavenge (SKAV-uhnj) to search for useful items

streamers (STREE-murz) people who broadcast themselves playing video games and talking online

Find Out More

BOOKS

Cunningham, Kevin. *Video Game Designer*. Ann Arbor, MI: Cherry Lake Publishing, 2016.

Powell, Marie. *Asking Questions About Video Games*. Ann Arbor, MI: Cherry Lake Publishing, 2016.

WEBSITES

Epic Games—Fortnite
www.epicgames.com/fortnite/en-US/home
Check out the official *Fortnite* website.

Fortnite Wiki
https://fortnite.gamepedia.com/Fortnite_Wiki
This fan-made website offers up-to-date information on the latest additions to *Fortnite*.

Index

balance, 14
Battle Royale mode,
    18–19, 29

crates, 11
Creative mode, 27–29
creativity, 21, 26–29

damage, 14, 28
destruction, 12–13,
    14, 16, 21, 25
developers, 14, 29

editing, 29

floors, 15–16, 17
flying, 28–29

grid, 15–16

hit points, 16

metal, 12, 15, 25
movement, 20–21,
    28–29

panic walls, 14, 22
pickaxe, 12–13
Port-a-Forts, 17
practice, 6, 19, 21,
    28

ramps, 14, 16, 21,
    22–23, 24–25, 29
roofs, 15–16

scavenging, 11–13,
    19–20, 22
stairs, 15–16, 29

stone, 12, 15, 25
storm, 22, 25
strategies, 9, 21,
    22
streamers, 4–5, 9
Supply Llamas, 11

towers, 17, 19–20,
    20–21, 23–24,
    25
traps, 17

walls, 13, 14, 15–16,
    20, 21, 22, 24, 25,
    29
weapons, 14, 16, 22,
    28
wood, 10–11, 12,
    13–14, 25

About the Author

Josh Gregory is the author of more than 125 books for kids. He has written about everything from animals to technology to history. A graduate of the University of Missouri–Columbia, he currently lives in Chicago, Illinois.